Killing
George Washington

Killing George Washington

THE AMERICAN WEST IN FIVE VOICES

Anne Jennings Paris

Killing George Washington:
The American West in Five Voices
Anne Jennings Paris

Copyright © 2009 by Anne Jennings Paris.
All rights reserved.

No part of this book may be reproduced or transmitted in any form or by any means, electronic or mechanical, including photocopying, recording, or by any information storage and retrieval system, without permission in writing from the publisher.

ISBN 13: 978-1-932010-30-5

Cover design by Kelley Dodd.
Interior design by Chelsea Harlan.
Text set in Caslon 540 LT Std and ITC Caslon 224 Std.

This publication is the product of Ooligan Press and the Publishing Program of the Center for Excellence in Writing at Portland State University. It was produced entirely by the students of this program. For credits, see back matter.

Ooligan Press
Portland State University
P.O. Box 751
Portland, OR 97207-0751
ooligan@ooliganpress.pdx.edu
www.ooliganpress.pdx.edu

Printed in the United States of America by Lightning Source.

This book is dedicated to my husband, Marc Paris.

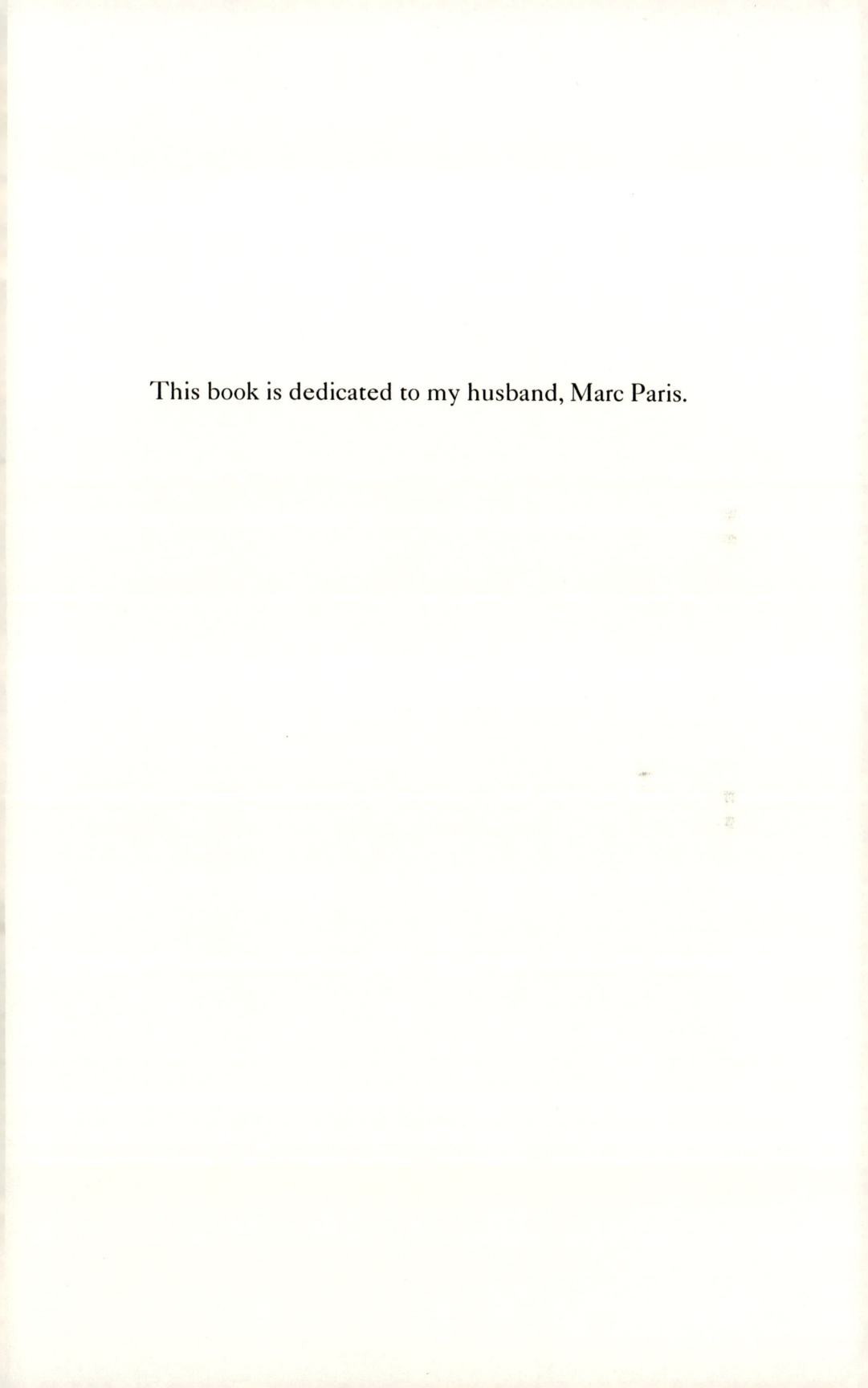

Acknowledgements

My husband Marc has supported me while I completed this book; more than anyone, he has my love, thanks, and appreciation. I thank the faculty, staff, and students of the San Jose State University English Department for their support, guidance, and camaraderie. My advisors Alan Soldofsky and John Engell deserve my special thanks. I also thank Al Young and Kristen Iversen, whose support fostered the earliest of these poems. Tiffany Ballard and Barbara Hall Blumer helped me get through the tough spots; Robert James and E. D. "Sweeney" Schragg offered ideas and inspiration; Eran Williams gave support and encouragement; and Kate Evans was the first gentle reader and editor of many of these poems. I owe thanks to Davis McCombs, whose book *Ultima Thule* inspired me, and to my father, Bruce Jennings, whose love of history and early stories about Lewis Wetzel fueled my interest in this subject. Finally, many thanks to everyone at Ooligan Press, especially Dennis Stovall, Karen Kirtley, Emilee Newman Bowles, and the students in the editing program for their careful attention to my work—I appreciated every note.

    Many other family members, friends, instructors, and strangers have assisted me on the path to completion of this project—some through their interest, some through their actions. Though I cannot thank each one individually, I thank them collectively.

Table of Contents

Lewis Wetzel 1

York 27

Charity Lamb 55

Ing Hay 75

Mary Elizabeth Jane Colter 105

Bibliography 132

Sometimes up out of this land
a legend begins to move.

—William Stafford

Lewis Wetzel

1763–1808

Indian Fighter

Lewis Wetzel was a hero. Lewis Wetzel was also a murderer. He was born in 1763, one of many children of a frontier family who settled near Wheeling Creek, in what is now West Virginia. Lewis Wetzel grew up learning how to be a master woodsman from his father. When he was about thirteen years old, Lewis was shot in the chest by a party of Indians (probably Wyandot), and he and his younger brother Jacob were abducted. They were later able to escape in spite of Lewis's injury.

After the abduction, Lewis Wetzel vowed to spend the rest of his life perfecting his fighting skills in order to ward off future dangers from Indian tribes. He became an Indian fighter and scout, leading families into the wilder portions of the American frontier to help them claim and establish their homesteads. But all of Lewis's vigilance and physical training did not help him prevent the death of his own father and brother at the hands of Indians on the Ohio River. These deaths were part of an ongoing, two-way exchange of killings between the white settlers and the Indian tribes along the American frontier.

After the death of his father and brother, Lewis Wetzel was more determined than ever to carry out his personal vendetta against all Indians. Many of his heroic deeds are recorded, such as saving a young bride from abduction and defending a fort against a major attack. What we do not know is the exact number of people Lewis Wetzel murdered. Though he often killed in self-defense, he also went in search of peaceful Indian parties to attack. Some historians and folklore experts speculate that Lewis killed more than one hundred people in his lifetime, usually as the unprovoked aggressor.

Today, Lewis Wetzel would be considered a serial killer or war criminal, but during his own lifetime, he was a popular figure, even though he was reportedly socially inept and preferred to talk to children or sit with the animals during community gatherings. His legendary abilities as a woodsman and "protector" of settlements made him a folk hero. But the political tide turned on Lewis Wetzel, and in 1791 he was sentenced to death for murdering George Washington, a "tame" Indian who was an ally of the territorial governor. Due to extreme pressure from the general public, Lewis Wetzel's death sentence was suspended on the condition that he depart the area, present-day Ohio.

In exile, Lewis traveled to New Orleans, where some accounts report that he spent time in prison, possibly because of involvement in a counterfeit ring or a duel over a woman; no definitive record exists about his life during this period. He later returned to his home in Wheeling Creek. He found the political climate much changed—his breed of rough-and-ready, blood-happy scout was no longer in favor. Somewhat aimless, Lewis continued to travel up and down the Ohio River and its territories before finally succumbing to yellow fever in 1808 in Natchez, Mississippi. He was buried in Mississippi, but in 1942, a Lewis Wetzel enthusiast had his body disinterred and buried in the McCreary Cemetery outside of Wheeling, West Virginia.

The McCreary Cemetery is a quiet, peaceful place—an unlikely resting place for a man consumed by such violence and hatred. I chose Lewis Wetzel as a subject for this book for two reasons. First, his story contains so many parallels to early twenty-first century politics. I began writing "his" poems in the months after September 11, when the news carried story after story of ordinary people transformed into brutal murderers and terrorists. I began to wonder—how was such a person made? And how do empires use individuals as scapegoats for their own brutality? Through Lewis Wetzel's story, I wanted to explore how acts of war may be perceived as murder or heroism depending on the lens we use to view them. I also wanted to consider how a person's nation could turn against him for the very acts and services it had once relied upon.

Second, and more personally, Lewis Wetzel is a relative of mine. Though he had no children of his own, his surviving siblings did. My mother's mother was a Wetzel and a descendant of that family. I remember hearing stories about Lewis Wetzel as I was growing up. My father often told me that Lewis Wetzel's long black hair and ability to run through the forest and reload his gun without stopping inspired James Fenimore Cooper's heroic character Natty Bumppo in *Deerslayer* and later novels. My father also told me that the Indians, frightened of Lewis Wetzel's stealthy presence in the forest, called him *Le Vent de la Mort*, which, translated from French, is "Deathwind." (The Huron—or Wyandot—federation of tribes learned French from their French allies in Canada before they migrated south into the Ohio River Valley.) The name Deathwind sounded so romantic to a young child listening to bedtime stories. But as I researched Lewis Wetzel for this book, I came to understand that "Indian fighter" was really a euphemism for Indian killer. Yet our national heroes, such as Presidents George Washington and Thomas Jefferson, depended on Indian fighters to open the frontier for white settlers.

In this era of political correctness, it is easy to characterize Lewis Wetzel as categorically evil, and I hope it goes without saying that I abhor his murderous acts. However, I hope to show in Lewis Wetzel's story and throughout this book that our nation was built not by angels or devils, but by whole, flawed people, one life at a time.

Notes on the Poems

From "The Raft"
Sassafrassed: The Wyandots who took Lewis Wetzel and his brother captive reportedly used a poultice of sassafras leaves to stem the blood flow from his gunshot wound. I was happy to have a reason to use sassafras in one of these poems about Wetzel. I remember, as a young girl, walking in the woods of West Virginia with my grandfather as he taught me what made sassafras trees so special: they have three distinct leaf shapes on the same tree. Later I learned that sassafras is the flavoring (now artificially reproduced) in root beer. It was only in researching this book that I learned that sassafras was used as a natural medicinal remedy.

From "Killing George Washington"
Harmar: General Josiah Harmar, tasked with organizing peace negotiations between the American government and local Indian tribes in present-day Ohio. Lewis Wetzel shot an Indian leader named Tegunteh, a favorite of Harmar's who went by the name of George Washington, while Tegunteh was traveling to the peace negotiations.

Kill Devil: Reportedly a name Lewis Wetzel had for his rifle. I find it fitting that he looked upon his gun as a living being, a friend, and a companion. We will see later in this book that Charity Lamb had a similar relationship with a gun, yet for quite different reasons.

From "*Le Vent de la Mort*"
Black Betty: A slang term for whiskey.

Breastbone

Who owns what is lost—God
or something darker? I've seen a devil
in the trees, his fingers stretched like roots
across the river valley. There's a war
and I don't know which side I'm on.

I was a boy when Indians shot me
and dragged me into wilderness.
The bullet took a piece of breastbone,
so I kept my hand on the hole, afraid
I'd bleed to death, till sleep caught me

and I drifted into shadow.
My soul leapt from my chest
and danced around the fire, then ran
into the woods, straggly and thin—
only half a soul, really.

Anew, I sprang to life, whispered, "Jacob,
brother, let's steal on home.
We can make the Ohio by dawn. We just
got to make the river." On the bank
a snake was rubbing off his skin.

I said, "Jacob, that's an omen
if I ever seen one." Then the Ohio
was running with blood, and I said,
"Jacob, that there's the apocalypse."
"Lewis," he said, "you gone crazy

with delirium." Jacob saw the hand
on the wounded chest. He didn't see
the snake and he didn't see the blood,
and he didn't see my shriveled soul
watching from the shore.

Now he's out, the poor devil can't get back in.
Stalking round my campfires—
I know what he's looking for.
He drifts behind the trees. When I sleep
he hovers over me, scraping at the scar.

If I wake, he hops and kicks
and scuttles toward the woods.
Some nights I yell, "Scat, demon!"
Other nights I'm lonesome, and damn
if he don't seem like good company.

He's looking for the breastbone,
that butterfly over the heart, that piece
they took from me. All this time, I don't tell him
he's looking in the wrong place:
they shot me in the cornfield.

Certain times before a storm, any burden
I have to carry, the rifle's recoil—all these
remind me of what's missing. All these echo
in the hollow place where the hole opened up
and my soul leapt out.

The Raft

At dawn with Jacob
on the branches and the logs
we'd cobbled together, I drifted
facedown, catching glimpses
of my eye between the cracks.

Blood seeped through my sassafrassed heart,
one drop and the river turned red
and calm and full of killing.
I heard the morning call of birds
across the water's edge,

and I said, "Yes, I'm crossing over."
Then I cared not for Virginia
or the corn or constant gloom
of forests, for the river was my bride,
and I was not afraid.

Scalp

Settlement men talk of peace, but my gun
points its finger toward the wilderness.
What I have witnessed must be atoned for:
my father gunned down in the border war,
his body full of bullet holes.

That day, a pact was sealed between us.
I have honed my body into an instrument
of terror—muscles tighten like ropes
against a straining animal—
the weapon I carry is my own heart.

If I strike them in their camps,
will they not hunt me in numbers?
My hair grows longer every year, drying
by the river's bank, the pelt of a sleek animal:
I become what they want to kill.

Killing George Washington

When Harmar called for red men
to make peace where the rivers join,
I answered my own call,
what I'd sworn to, lived by, a day
no different from any other.

And the night before the killing
wasn't what you'd call unusual—
no stars with tails, no blotting of the moon,
all the rivers ran the right direction,
and the sun was courteous in its coming.

I waited by the roadside for red men to pass.
Didn't matter who, just doing my part,
as the sun did by rising, as the river did by flowing,
as the blood did by spilling.
All the Lord's servants working together.

Kill Devil bucked in my hands like a colt at the gate—
the Indian fell from his horse.
My tomahawk leapt for its prize,
and I took the scalp for my belt to honor the Lord.
But that bastard didn't die, not at first.

Harmar came running from his fort,
knelt beside the breathing corpse, crying,
"George Washington, who was it killed you?"
I knew something was wrong then, if a red beast
was wearing a great man's name.

George was a long-winded bastard. But his breath and my name were the same: *Le Vent de la Mort.* At last Death did his part. You see how it went wrong, how this killing was every bit the same, but this time the white men turned and called it murder.

The Trial at Fort Washington

Judge John Cleve Symmes was a fine-looking man
but I found his aspect the worried kind,
like he feared a ha'nt or spirit coming up behind.
He wore a new coat and a knotted tie, but had skin

redder than an apple. That's how I knew
he was part of this country, of a sort
to do right. I spoke in his court,
tried to make him see what was true:

You say this Indian came for peace,
calling himself George Washington.
Then say I've done not murder, but treason.
For if all a red man needs to call peace

in this Ohio Territory
is to take the name of his enemy, why then,
I have killed all our upper statesmen.
Declare war against me.

They say I murdered the Indian.
If so, Judge, then say I murdered
not one brutal beast, but one hundred.
I'm a hunter, not a subtle man.

Explain the finer points of peace and war.
Five Indians round a campfire: if I pass on
and tomorrow, they kill your woman,
who will comfort you? General Harmar?

What does he offer that satisfies?
A paper treaty? A fort protected by the slow,
muddy Muskingum, and the mighty Ohio?
I've watched the rivers run into your territories.

I know what waits there for your people.
Go once into that wilderness alone
and bring with you your woman,
your sons in their light cradles.

In the night, what god will you pray to?
Will you hope the cradles turn to coffins?
Or that the savage hearts will soften,
take your boys, and raise them up to slay you?

Then maybe you'll begin to understand
the arrowhead pointed at my breast
since I first drank mother's milk. Rest?
There's none. Killing, that's the price of land.

Ohio

During dry spells you could walk across her.
My feet knew the stones by heart.
She was my river, and I drank her, slept beside her,
bled into her. I started to feel

the river was in me somehow, blue
under my skin. Then I knew, it ain't enough
to know the start of a river, nor the middle neither—
you got to know the ending, too.

So I followed her. When I'd meet a man,
he'd say, "Where you headed?"
"Ohio River," I'd say. Man liked telling me,
"This here's the Mississippi. Y'all done missed it."

Some folks like to say you done wrong
and some folks think naming a thing makes it so.
But I knew my river by the taste of her,
the taste of my brother and father, too.

Man don't forget his own blood,
just cause it goes around calling itself some other name.
Where her water sings, that's where I'm found.
She whispers my way down, Natchez, New Orleans,

ocean-bound. When I saw her spilling
to the sea like that, I wondered did she run
the whole world round? Ohio, if I fell into your arms
would you carry me home?

The Huntsman after New Orleans

I was confused by city talk, the ladies'
turning heads was something I could hardly see
for what it was—small gold coins in tiny hands—
I didn't know the ways—

(He never takes his hand from the barrel of the gun.)

do you want me to say I lived like a dog?
It was worse—naked, two years on the black stone
of the jail. Say it was women, or dirty money.
In truth, I got lost without my, my—

(He's disoriented, scratches at a scar on his chest.)

hatred will spur a man beyond love,
the one the birthing of the other,
a marriage—if you want to call it that.
I loved so that I hated, and I hated
so that I lived.

(He drinks.)

After I was freed, I never moved the same.
I don't mean on the outside, mind, though I was weak.
But the inside engine that powered the will,
the hunger, had been left like a fire
untended through the night.

(He leans forward, teeth rotted, neck tight and knotted.)

I waited for the taste to rise again.
I waited and watched the empty woods, the shadows
our mouths had made. I moved through the trees
wondering what had become of my prey,
what had become of me.

At the Tavern

I hear a rising wind
like a scream before a killing.
I use a flintlock rifle, a tomahawk,
a knife, or nothing more
than my bare hands.

Once, to get a hundred-dollar bounty,
I walked two hundred miles for one kill.
Some say I carried a good thing too far.
There's a lot folks can say
from inside a settlement wall.

Most times, I wait till they're on me,
up close, then shoot. Mind, I don't sit there
like an old buck waiting for an arrow.
I'm in the trees, taking my measure,
using my wit. That's why God made trees.

In the summer, the whole world turns forest,
and mine's the first foot on a place.
I'm the goddamned first American,
I get to thinking—solitude, that's peace,
not some treaty in a stranger's fist.

I never knew that Indian, see,
doesn't mean I didn't hate him. Fear—
yours, I mean—that's why I'm here, son.
You're the damned reason I'm here.
Think about that while you drink your whiskey.

The Taste of Blood

Once I got careless and captured.
An old man begged them let me go—
seems he forgot the taste of blood.
The young ones hollered and kicked him
till he crept like a dog to the trees.

The young men fixed the stake
while women gathered firewood,
and I asked my God for a swift end.
All as it should be.

Then the old dog came sneaking
from the forest to my feet.
He spirited me away on a horse.
Who ever heard of a dog on a horse?
When he freed me, I shot him.

Le Vent de la Mort

If I had a hound dog, I'd call him Shawnee,
but this here Kill Devil makes fine company.
Yes, I got me a gun instead, my boy,
I got me a gun instead.

> *O where, O where is Black Betty?*
> *I want to kiss her sweet lips.*

Preacher says vengeance belongs to the Lord,
but God's up in heaven and I'm in this world,
so I go to kill in His stead, my boy,
I go to kill in His stead.

> *O fetch me a glass of Black Betty!*
> *I want to kiss her sweet lips.*

Some say I've been marked since the day I was born,
and some say when I'm dead I'll still scream from my tomb,
'cause I am *le vent de la mort*, my boy,
I am *le vent de la mort*.

> *So drink, drink to Black Betty!*
> *I'm dying to kiss her sweet lips.*

The Story of Lena Crow

I been saving this story for a time when I might feel something by it. Four girls lay sleeping. Come morning only one woke—the others bludgeoned in their beds. Folks found Lena hiding out behind the corncrib, gone mute.

This, in a time when I still felt something at the sight of a crushed skull, the bits of bone and blood that mingled with the girls' long hair, as black as the crow.

After the peace, some Indians came begging for food. Lena, her tongue restored, recognized her sisters' bridegrooms. Her brothers did what was right.

Some might say a man like me has no faith. I got *only* faith, the justice I believe in, the sanctity of death, the right to die for your sins.

You believe what you will. I'm tired of stories—the captors, the victims—all the same. All were saved, all died. What else is there to tell?

My mother tried to teach me language, but the longer I live, the stranger words feel on my tongue, and the more the company of men fills me with a certain terror.

Deathwind

For forty years, I carried death close to me—
the bullet in my chest returned
with the tides, and the blood from my gun
flooded the banks of the Ohio.
Then the fever come.

Now they whisper my name to babies
who suckle at red breasts.
I am the lullaby that rocks them to sleep—
my gun, the report of thunder,
my bullet, the lightning's flash.

I run through the trees in the night,
calling to the living, calling to the dead—
I am the wind that rides at the warrior's back,
the ghost of the Empire, the great white wave—
I am the death that comes for the red man.

Invocation

You want my stories to come out songs,
I'd rather fiddle while you dance
than sing another word. History wants
to leave me, lose me, plain unspeak me.

    (Let his story fit my breath—)

If I had a song, I'd sing the river, the words
for stones, I'd sing the trees, the words for trees,
the ways of trees, I'd hold the trees
in my mouth like a word,

    (Let there be a haunting refrain—)

hold the river in my mouth like a word,
hold my brother in my mouth like a word,
hold my father in my mouth like a word,
my mother, my mouth, my word.

    (Look to the grave, the grassy stones—)

You wonder where the mystery lies, or maybe
you said my story lies. Let this be a book of death,
and let's record each act of killing, a history
worthy of recalling each man, each eye,

    (He's ranting now, or does he glorify?)

each final breath 'neath fallen tree.
I offered everything to death—
I gave back childhood, speaking less,
feeling more, turned animal.

    (Write that. Animal. No, don't. He's—)

Now I'm the one the animal fears. What is the word
for what I am? I live by cycles of the moon, I fit
the hardness of the earth. I haven't been invented yet.
Don't ask again. I'm tired of talking, listen—

    (A wind is rattling the bones—)

let's get to fiddling now, I'll play the song,
the one you like with the little boy,
where everybody ends up dead.
You make the words, I'll be the tune,
and I'll be moving in the trees.

York

1770s–1834(?)

Slave

York was a slave owned by William Clark of Lewis and Clark fame. York was born just a few years after Clark, who was born in 1770. In those days, young masters and slave children often played together, so it is likely that the two boys were friends even before York was chosen to become Clark's "body servant." This title meant that York attended to Clark morning, noon, and night. "Body servant" was a relatively high position within the plantation slave community and would have entitled York to the relative luxuries of better food and nicer clothing.

During the Lewis and Clark Expedition, York served as a full member of the Corps of Discovery: he hunted food, poled the keelboat along the Missouri River, carried his fair share during exhausting portages, and even had his private parts nearly frozen off during a brutal winter in the Bitterroot Mountains. Unlike the other men who accompanied the Lewis and Clark Expedition, York received no land or compensation as reward for his efforts as a member of the party. Upon return from the Pacific Ocean, York asked Clark for his freedom; Clark said no.

Little is known about York's personal life. He could not read or write and therefore left no record of himself. Most of what we know about him comes from the journals and letters that Meriwether Lewis and William Clark wrote during and after the expedition. Much of what Clark wrote incriminates himself: he resented York for seeking his freedom and planned to rent him out to a brutal master as punishment.

We know York was married. If he was married prior to the departure of the Expedition, he would have been separated from his wife for the length of the journey (about three years). When he returned, York asked Clark to assign him to a job near his wife, who was owned by another family. But Clark only allowed him a brief visit, then required that York return to Clark's side. Soon after, York's wife was "sold down the river" to Mississippi, and it is likely York never saw her again.

Reports differ about York's ultimate fate. Some historians believe Clark kept York enslaved until his death by cholera, hiring him out to brutal masters as punishment for his continued requests for freedom. Some say Clark finally freed York and set him up in business hauling freight with a horse and cart, but that York failed at the business and was planning to ask for Clark's renewed patronage when he died.

However, in 1832, a man traveling to the Rocky Mountains reported seeing a black man who called himself York living as a chief among the Crow Indians. This York claimed to have traveled to the Pacific and back with Lewis and Clark, and to have later escaped to freedom.

The questions that linger about York's fate make him an intriguing figure. Did he perish from sickness, worn down by his enslavement; or did he run free on the prairies, revered and at ease? I found it impossible to take a stand on his fate. My guess is that he died from cholera, but the romantic vision of him, living as a Crow chief, is too tempting for me to give up. And so I chose to leave York forever at the crossroads of history. You can make up your own mind.

As for the form of these poems, I wanted to create a parallel to the famous journals of Lewis and Clark. Because York could not read or write, I imagined him creating "oral journal entries" of his experiences, both during the journey and afterward.

Notes on the Poems

From "Two-Self"
Two-Self: A term used by William Clark in his journals to describe his relationship with York.

Arikara: An Indian tribe visited by the Corps of Discovery. Pronounced *uh*-**rik**-er-*uh*.

From "Wintering in St. Louis"
Collins and Hall: Members of the Corps of Discovery.

Seaman: Reports differ as to whether Meriwether Lewis's dog was named Scannon or Seaman. More resources refer to him as Seaman.

From "Megalonyx"
Petit chien: Early French traders coined this term—literally translated as "little dog"—for prairie dogs because of their bark-like call.

When I met him: There is no actual recorded meeting between York and President Thomas Jefferson.

From "Fort Clatsop"
Fort Clatsop: During the winter of 1805–1806, the Corps of Discovery camped at a site they named Fort Clatsop, located by the mouth of the Columbia River near Astoria, Oregon.

Quamash: Also known as *camas*, an ornamental blue flowering plant with an edible root.

Mandan: The Corps of Discovery spent their first winter with the Mandan people near the upper Missouri River.

Invocation

Path winding into wilderness, I invoke you.
Shrouded figure at the crossroads, I invoke you.
Two-headed history, I invoke you:
a country stretches before us, shimmering highway,
city lights bejewel the plains,
the Walmarts, the wigwams, the all-night diners,
the happy endings we've been waiting for,
riding high in our U-Hauls filled with the furniture
our parents gave us, the boxes of Polaroids, pot lids,
and Tupperware—the life we've worked to acquire.

O virgin nation opening to worthy men, I invoke you.
Figure in my American landscape, perched on the brink
   of possibility,
forever pregnant with your own mastery, I invoke you:
shrug off the cholera, slip the bonds of death,
take up where legend left off!
I'll look for you in the high altitudes of memory,
where monuments to ourselves dot the landscape—
too late to discover you, I'll make you what I want you
   to be.

Two-Self

Before I was Big Medicine
I was William's boy.
I danced for the mistress,
turning cartwheels by the big house,
wanting to be chosen.

After that I wore a full suit
of tow linen and talked like him
until in the dark, you couldn't tell
where William ended and I began.

When he told me to, I danced
for the Arikara, my shirt off
in the firelight.
They touched me, touched my skin,
after the months I'd spent alone
among white men.

When he hunts the river's edge,
I carry his gun. The buffalo
we carry home together.
Nights, I swim to the sandy bar
to pick watercress for his dinner.

How many times have I held
the razor to his throat?
How many times has he called me
his boy? Some twenty summers,
I have kept his body;
he belongs to me, and I to him.

Juba

My sister raised her fist
when she was born,
and rejected the breast,
her gums like tiny teeth.
Monday's child,
they named her Juba.
I haven't seen her
near twenty years.

My mother told
of an African king,
his infancy
a trophy of war.
Raised among Caesars,
he shone like a jewel
in white marble.
He learned to read and write,
returned to rule,
a slave king.

I can't put pen to paper,
but I know what it means
to sleep in the master's house,
to dream my sister's sharp
white teeth, her full-grown fist.

Wintering in St. Louis

Collins got drunk and Hall
with him, tapping whiskey
they were meant to guard.
The other men did the flogging,
gleeful, drunk themselves
on the feel of leather.

I watched from the hut
as the lash struck skin,
a hundred for Collins,
fifty for Hall.

The dog, Seaman,
crouched by Captain Lewis,
his whimpering veiled
by the shrieks of white men.

At first he barked
till he tired of his own pleading
and surrendered to the blood,
his head bent
against the leg of his master.

What We Brought

We stowed the promise of trade
in canvas sacks, stacked
on the bottom of the keelboat.
Each sack bore the markings of a tribe,
the names we called them by.

Our coming meant yards
of red flannel, mirrors, awls,
brass kettles, and ivory combs.
What they wanted—rifles,
powder, balls—we did not give;
instead, we showed our own.

Captain Lewis Speaks

"Children," he called them. "Children,
your New White Father will provide for you."
From a sack he pulled pointed hats
and coats of red lace.
Then he passed out coins—
Jefferson on one side, two hands
clasped on the other.
The chiefs talked, their heads bent
under the weight of the hats.
Then, coins flashing in their hands,
they turned and asked for whiskey.

The Bear

Around Indian fires,
children ran from me,
so I charged to make them squeal
and fall down laughing.

William cried, "Bear, I tame you,"
so I came to his place and lay
under his power, my body
bent to his will.

We had played this as boys
dreaming of what lay beyond our farm.
The land felt large to us then,
the horizon a kingdom
for other princes.

But I find him lord of me
here as well—the rivers,
the mountains, the lines he draws
on maps do not break
his sovereign will or might.

At noon he surveys the sun,
at night the moon, king even
of their coming and going.
And he it is who names the star,
the bright fixed point
we move against.

Big Medicine

They'd never seen a skin so black,
even among my own people.
A squaw led me to her lodge
while her husband kept watch:
he too wanted good fortune,
big medicine.

She tasted my skin, tried to rub
the blackness from me. If wanting
could have washed me clean,
I'd have been white since boyhood;
I'd have saved myself in the cricks
of Virginia and risen from the water
freezing, free.

White Pelicans

August—a blanket of white
embraced the water
till we floated soundless
on its soft breast. A bend
in the river revealed
thousands of them,
preening and grooming
with waggling beaks.
They fluttered and breathed
on the sandbar, a sea
of white, till the Captain
aimed his rifle at the center
and fired, and they lifted
to the air, a mass of wings
and feathers, a shattered angel
confused by thunder
on a cloudless day.

Coyote

He watched me from the shore,
and together we saw the August moon
dipping herself into the waters of the Missouri.
His fur went white in the darkness,
and I was afraid when he called me *brother*.

The next day, he trailed us, and I saw him
rolling in the tall grass beside the river.
William called the Captain when he spied him,
saying, *Something for your specimen collection.*

That prairie wolf, I said,
he don't aim to get killed tonight.
That so? said William. *Well, I aim to kill him.*
Only one of us will come away satisfied.

We took to shore, my gun in the lead.
I walked heavy in my boots and rustled my arms against
    the tall grasses.
Coyote ran into the deep prairie,
laughing between his teeth.

My Name

On the river they named places
for each other, for the dog,
for me. *York's Eight Islands*,
York's River, the first ownership
I'd been allowed. To own so much
at once! My mouth tightened
around the sounds of possession.

Megalonyx

All day, as we poled the keelboat
through churning water,
Captain Lewis combed the shores
for specimens, suspending
leaf and bird, the *petit chien*,
in boxes to be carried back
to Jefferson.

When I met him, the President
took a book from the shelf
and turned to the skeleton
of an ancient beast, raised
on its haunches.

Megalonyx, he called it,
that name his own invention.
*Who knows what we may find
across the prairies?* he said.
*A mountain of salt
along Missouri's banks.
Volcanoes in the Badlands.*

I watched Captain Lewis turn
powder to ink and scratch his notes
on two kinds of paper,
a thousand words
for the head of a bird.

But I collected nameless
wind across the grasses, the space
between land and sky
that could not be catalogued,
its bones laid open to the great man.

Walking-Off Place

The West is a walking-off place.
Whole villages move
with the river, with the weather.
They leave their ghosts in empty towns.

Our own man Shannon went missing.
Three days Captain Lewis worried
till we found him on the shore
waiting to rejoin his kind.

Up where the waters divide
we wandered, skins withering on bone.
I feared I'd stagger
off the rocky, bitter teeth.

Then I got a notion
that freedom must feel this way,
a single choice—walk on
or drop into the sky.

Fort Clatsop

I woke from slavery to a dream
of winter—eternal rain,
the rushing of waves against the shore
with hardly any whiskey left to share.
Still, the redskins offered women to keep us warm,
and by the heat of their skin,
I measured my being.

One man taught me
to make a drum from elk's hide.
How we tired of elk!
Elk and rain. I longed
for the Mandan corn,
the blue fields of quamash
that rippled like an oasis
in brown valleys.

One day a great fish washed onshore.
I ran past the salt-making hut
to see the beast lying black
and still against the sand.
I'd imagined him with scales
like the beasts I'd seen
on William's maps.

But he was soft,
skin covered in whiskers,
barnacles, and rime.
One man kicked him,
others cut his flesh with knives.
Seabirds pecked in the eddies
of his body. He seemed to breathe.
His eye bulged, dangerous and wet.

Homefire

I must have looked changed to them,
body hardened by the Bitterroots,
muscles fed on the flesh of buffalo,
the pink rush of salmon.
But could they see beneath my skin,
the strange new self I carried
to my mother's hearth—
that I had been three years a man, and nothing more?
While women hurried to prepare a feast,
I told my tales around the fire, tongue
tripping on freedom. They crowded me
like ghosts from another life, black faces
feeding on a sudden terror.

My Wife

I dream her body some nights, the curve of her
stolen and held against me, a stranger.
She has gone to Natchez and won't be back
this lifetime. I wonder what she carried
in her womb and what new husband she found
in that deep, dark country.
Mornings come hard, so I close my eyes
and watch the grasses swim the prairies,
hear the drip of oars as they travel between strokes.
What is freedom, now she is gone?
A vast ocean, discovered, unrevealing.

Returned from a Far Country

We met a woman by that name.
If I'd known her language,
I'd have caught her behind a tree
saying, "How will I come home again
now the spray of the Pacific
has salted this skin?"

In the heart of the Bitterroots,
I named myself Source of All Rivers—
I had straddled the divide,
the water of two worlds in my veins—
I walked behind my master yet I chose it.
His skin sagged like mine around his bones,
and the cold cut us both the same.

When I returned to the home place,
I named myself the River's Secret,
for I knew the distant riddle
of Missouri's source, freedom
won and lost when I looked
from the top of the world.

But when I pass over Jordan,
who shall I be then?
When my body drops to bones,
will I feel the terrible bite of freedom,
as I slip alone into God's wilderness?
Tell me, how will I go home,
and what will my name be when I die?

Hired–Out

Captain Lewis is dead.
I heard through stories
how he cut himself with razors
after bullets failed, and said,
I am so strong; it is so hard to die.
The world he found was not enough to fill him.

Emptiness welcomed each of us home.
I grieved for William, his great heart
still beating. Today we are so far apart,
I think we may not be reconciled,
and two will be two forever. Friend,
in death, I wonder, will you meet him
somewhere beyond the Pacific?
And will I meet you?

Charity Lamb

181?–1879

Pioneer

CHARITY LAMB WAS OREGON'S FIRST convicted murderess. She bashed her husband Nathaniel's head in with an axe. At the trial, prosecutors claimed she was in love with a drifter named Collins, and that she killed Nathaniel so that she and her teenage daughter Mary Ann could run away to California to reunite with her lover. Charity's defense argued that Nathaniel was a wife beater who had threatened to kill Charity many times, including his compelling threat to shoot her the very morning of the murder. Newspapers at the time of her trial characterized Charity as a monster and warned men that if she went free, she might serve as an example to the wives and daughters of Oregon, who would start hacking folks up left and right without fear of punishment.

The jurors at Charity's trial convicted her of second-degree murder, and due to mandatory sentencing laws, Judge Cyrus Olney sentenced her to life in prison.

Charity's early life is largely undocumented. One of her descendants has been diligently researching and documenting Charity's family tree and believes Charity was born in either southern Virginia or northern North Carolina. After Charity married Nathaniel, the pair became lifelong pioneers, moving first to Indiana, then to Missouri, and finally, to Oregon. During that time, Charity gave birth to at least six children.

Charity killed Nathaniel soon after arriving in Oregon, no doubt worn out and worn down by the Oregon Trail and Nathaniel's brutality. It was reported at the trial that she carried his gun with her along the trail to Oregon to stop him from using it against her, indicating that violence was an ongoing problem in Charity and Nathaniel's marriage.

Charity's children testified that Nathaniel had beaten her many times and once threw a hammer at her, wounding her in the head.

After the trial, Charity spent two years in the Oregon City jail, then became prisoner number eight at the newly built penitentiary on the outskirts of Portland. There, she did hard labor, washing clothes for the other prisoners and the warden's family. All the men convicted of second-degree murder in the same time period were let go within two years of sentencing due to overcrowding. Charity was never released. Instead, after eight years in prison, she was transferred to the Oregon Asylum, run by the reportedly kind and forward-thinking Dr. James Hawthorne. Asylum records show that she died in 1879 of "apoplexy"—a term referring to what we would now call a stroke or hemorrhage. At the time of her death, Charity Lamb had been incarcerated for twenty-five years.

Dr. Hawthorne, a generous man, was reported to pay for the burial of his indigent patients. The cost of burial at the time was about ten dollars. I like to believe Charity was a beneficiary of this final kindness and was laid to rest in the Lone Fir Cemetery with the other deceased inmates for company, near the plot Hawthorne later chose for his own burial. If so, her grave remains undiscovered.

These days, there's a doggie daycare and a brew pub on the site of the old asylum. The old prison is long since gone, and new condos and trendy shops line the waterfront. The old Lamb homestead is now part of a privately held parcel of land near Eagle Creek, just beyond Oregon City.

Notes on the Poems

From "In the Madhouse"
A city bringing light to the edge of the wilderness: Oregon City, the first city incorporated west of the Mississippi River. Charity Lamb and her family settled on the outskirts of this town, which is still recognized as the official "End of the Oregon Trail." The main industry in town was steamboat construction. Just after the Lamb family arrived, Oregon City was the site of a major tragedy: the boiler on the steamboat *Gazelle* exploded, killing at least twenty-five people and injuring at least thirty.

From "Mary Ann"
The Falls: Willamette Falls in Oregon City.

The Sentence

On sentencing day, I see a bird caught up short
in a fence, head pointed toward the ground,
clawed feet in twisted wire. The jailer leads me to court,
my wrists rubbed raw by iron bands.

Cyrus Olney, the judge, hunches like an owl
on his perch. He doesn't want me to hang
but says it was my duty to flee, not kill.
The jury hisses like a knot of snakes.

I am old, and the tabloids draw me older—
wizened hands, veins bulging under skin—
but not too old to nurse my young. "Murder
in the second degree," declares the foreman.

A stranger pries the baby from my breast,
Prisley's tiny hand grabs air. I can't breathe.
Milk stain spreads across the front of my dress,
shackles come clawing at my hands. Wait! Please!

Am I really so different from other wives?
Every day, I suffered a new shame,
kept quiet to save my life, my children's lives.
Mothers, don't tell me you wouldn't do the same—

soul deadened by your husband's fist,
your hand grasping for the moment's weapon,
choking on the bitter taste of what he promised:
my husband was going to kill me! Listen!

Invocation

It's raining again, Charity, a soft November rain,
trees swathed in green moss, leaves piled on lawns.
Gentle wind blowing in, a storm about to begin,
the radio says. Out by the river, crumbling stones

of your cabin erode. Descendants cull
records, post messages on the internet,
try to find themselves in your line. A strip mall
abuts Lone Fir Cemetery's 10,000 unknown dead:

are you one of them? The rain drizzles
constantly, softens the sound of excavators.
Over there, a fresh pile of roses
wreathed in Cyrillic characters—

new pioneers buried where old firs have grown
over grave markers, marble phaged into trunk.
I walk, scraping leaves off modest stones.
I've been looking for you in trees, in rocks.

Charity, come haunt the woods behind my house.
America is the god that drove you,
and I need a muse—
come. Come show me how to love you.

A Man, a Gun

Smooth Virginia summer. A man stumbles
over words. He has spoken to Father, he has planned,
saved. He promises to provide for me, mumbles
about future children. Reaches for my hand.

Was that me? Was that him? I thought I was grown!
Maybe it's not too late to untie this thread,
unspool the miles of trail, throw down
the meals of salt pork, the crusts of bread,

peel off the scars from his hammer blows,
wipe him from between my legs, return the children
to my womb. Too late! While I sleep, the man grows
cruel with drink. The dream is at an end.

So I walk in unknown country, carrying his gun.
If I don't, the man might use it against me.
In the stretch between Missouri and Oregon,
the gun becomes another limb, an extension of my body.

And so the gun bolsters me, drives me on—
sleep against it, hold it closer than a babe, don't let it stray.
The man revels in my courtship with his gun:
our union sanctions his madness—he owns me.

Can a mother love a weapon like a child?
My girl shrinks and watches me with careful eyes.
My boys mock me, think I've gone trail sick, wild.
But all along, I am saving their lives.

I've heard men tell stories round the campfire
about a fiend who steals a body's life and breath.
Each year, the man hardens, while I grow weaker.
I walk the days holding fast to death.

The Rose Quartz Woman

Mother gave me a secret gift when I wed—
a lady wrapped in swirling ribbons, her hair piled
on her head, a rabbit tamed on her palm, carved
all in rose quartz. How I loved it as a child!

At night, I pull the woman from her box. She's pale
and unblemished as moonlight, as love should be.
Even on the trail, I hid her from Nathaniel.
He's fond of taking all my pleasures from me.

Now he says he'll take my boys south, says he'll wait
till the milk-cow has her calf, then take her along.
I want to scream, "A mother is more than a teat!"
But I'm silent, betrayed by a fearful tongue.

He plans to cleave me from my children for good,
raise them up in his image, as he sees fit.
Today, he drives me off into the woods,
taunts me with the gun and tells me, "Git!"

I want to be the rose quartz woman, tranquil,
strong. Instead I am the rabbit, cowering, scared.
"Kill your woman later," I hear our neighbor yell.
"We got a bear to hunt!" They laugh, and I'm spared.

Something new crawls from the brush, hardened and mute.
He'll be gone till supper, so there's time to search the shed,
time to put the house in order while it's still light,
time to wrap my hair in ribbons, pile it high on my head.

Thirsty

For a while, I'm running, I'm being chased—
by a bear with blood-matted fur. No, not a bear,
a man. A man is chasing me, his hand is raised,
asking for something. What is he asking for?

Now I am wandering the river alone.
My hand was holding something heavy, I think,
but not now. Now it is empty as the moon—
a deer bends to the river, bends down to drink,

see how the deer is thirsty—not a deer,
no, a woman. I am afraid someone will shoot
the woman. "Run!" I scream, but she drinks the river.
A person calls to me from a house. "You alright,

Mrs. Lamb?" The person is Mrs. Smith—yes—
she is Mrs. Smith and I am Mrs. Lamb.
"Charity, what's happened? There's blood on your dress."
"Nathaniel shot a bear," I say. Now men have come.

One says, "A gash in his head from front to rear,
five inches long, through the bone. He's a goner."
Are they talking about the man or the bear?
Mrs. Smith puts me in a chair by the fire.

"Your husband is dying," she says, "and your son
needs to eat." I feel my breasts, rock-hard with milk,
breaking my heart. One of the men loads his gun.
Mrs. Smith takes my arm. "It's a long walk

home," she says. I'm afraid. The men walk ahead.
I don't want them to see the woman in the river—
she's gone and got the bloody axe from our shed.
"The axe was thirsty," she cries, "just like the deer."

Life

Condemned, bound in a wagon, brought downriver
to the grandest prison west of the Mississippi.
The warden calls me his model prisoner.
My cell is dank—there's a spider for company.

I'm the only woman here. Men with greater sins
go free, while I scrub the floors, do their laundry.
The spider shows me how to live. She spins
while I labor to keep the memories at bay.

Stir the boiling pot, wring water from the clothes.
Grease and sweat settle in the roots of my hair.
I think my blood is full of lye, my skin grows
powdery. No one touches me anymore.

Nights are the worst, lying in the damp, dark cell.
I hear voices drift in from the taverns. I try
not to think of Mary Ann singing, the yeast smell
of Prisley's hair, Thomas's sweet, shy

look at the trial. The spider spins her strands
of silvery gray, my hair shot through with age.
Years run like quicksilver through my hands—
I wake up cold as a razor's edge.

In the Madhouse

We have all races here: Chinamen, savages,
Jews. Some with syphilis, the rest insane.
A comforting fog creeps 'round the edges
of rooms. I don't believe in anything but rain.

Here we have milk and sweets brought to us on trays
and a garden full of food someone else tends.
Water runs in iron pipes through the house.
I can drift for days while memory sends

me upriver. First time I saw Willamette Falls,
I thought how far we'd come, just to meet up
in that moment. Even then I was part crazy.
I wanted to empty myself like a cup,

spill the past into the river. "Mary Ann,"
I said, "We are witnessing the sacred."
I knew right then there was something to believe in—
maybe it was America, maybe God.

All the people, all the water, rushing to this point,
and I was a part of it—me—Charity.
At last, I thought, maybe I had a reason
for the walking, for the bleeding: a city

bringing light to the edge of the wilderness.
Then, in April, just above town, a steamboat
blew bodies into the air, thirty men, a bloody mess
of arms and legs, a thousand pieces left afloat,

swept over the churning falls. For days the air
that drifted to our cabin smelled of charred wood
and flesh. Pretty soon, nothing seemed to matter.
In a world without God, what was one more man dead?

Near me, now, the doctors and the inmates play.
Voices like children call me back to the madhouse.
New men and women arrive here every day—
already, they build more rooms to hold us.

**A Note about My Burial,
to Be Given to Dr. Hawthorne upon My Death**

If I don't think of the past, then I am free,
and this asylum becomes a kind of haven,
or is it heaven? Maybe I have died already.
But no, the Quakers come remind me of my sin.

"Lady, repent! It's not too late!" they hiss.
If they had sticks, they'd poke me like a caged freak,
make me squirm. But I want this wilderness
called madness—it was my crime, my choice to make.

If you cut me open, my blood would trace
a map from Virginia clear to Oregon,
missed turnoffs petering out in high places,
all roads, all rivers leading to this destination.

So throw my body in the ground with no headstone.
When the curious come looking for a ghost,
they'll find the fallen needles of the lone fir,
silent acre of madmen, silent breath of the past.

Or if there must be a stone, let earth and tree and flood
conspire to cover my name, let my bones grow
tangled and brittle as reeds and sink beneath the mud,
and then let me go, let me go, let me go.

Mary Ann

Mary Ann, love of my life, last trial to bear.
If I can write her, maybe I can die,
like a river goes on striving for an uncertain shore,
like a person walks across a whole country

to atone. She is half his blood, half his drive.
If I could strip that portion from her, I would.
Turns out, I'm the one person I cannot forgive
for making her live this life, for spreading his seed.

I knew by Missouri—my husband would never stay,
would rather leave pieces of his family on the trail
until land stopped. By driving us, he'd never die.
He'd sow a whole nation of Nathaniel

one territory at a time. Taking wood, soil, water,
leaving shacks behind him and husked out wagon hulls.
He never wanted a home for us. He wanted to conquer
the land, collect offspring like the skins of dead animals.

Because she shares my sex, maybe Mary Ann
will share the inclinations of my blood.
Am I cruel to wish her more murderess than man?
Killing Nathaniel was an act of love.

We'd come so far together; she grew up on the trail,
and I breathed America's dirt until I became it.
I like to remember her standing near the Falls,
skirts held above the mud, witness to something sacred.

A man loves his country for what he ain't done yet,
a woman for what she's already done.
I feel something coming, a rush of blood to the head,
the sweet taste of iron on my tongue.

Ing Hay

1862–1952

Healer

"Doc" Ing Hay was a young Chinese immigrant who, during the later years of the Oregon gold rush, became one of the West's most respected healers. He was born in 1862 in the village of Hsia Pin Li in Taishan County, Guangdong Province. Like most young Chinese men of his time, Ing Hay married early and already had a son and a daughter by the age of twenty-one. In all probability, his parents arranged his marriage; he would have been under great pressure to produce children (especially a son) to carry on the family line and take care of the elders when they were no longer able to work.

Taishan County was the birthplace of most of the early Chinese immigrants to America. Beset by ongoing civil war, famine, overcrowding, and devastating epidemic disease, the Taishanese were desperate to seek a living elsewhere. Ing Hay and his father came to America in 1883. At first they settled in Walla Walla, Washington, most likely working as gold miners in the largely played-out gold fields. In 1887, Ing Hay's father returned home to China, but Ing Hay decided to stay. After meeting another young Taishanese "visitor" (as the Chinese called themselves) named Lung On, Ing Hay moved to John Day, Oregon, where Lung On knew of a business opportunity. The two men became business partners in creating Kam Wah Chung, a grocery store and doctor's office that mostly served the Chinese community in the busy mining and ranching town.

Little is known about how Ing Hay acquired medical training. Perhaps he studied under Dr. Lee, an established practitioner of Chinese medicine in San Francisco's thriving Chinatown. What is known is that Doc Hay proved to be a natural at diagnosing a person's illness by feeling his or her pulse. Doc Hay's record of saving a reported six thousand lives earned him legendary status across the Northwest. This reputation allowed him to cross over into white society at a time when most Chinese were kept at a distance, either as domestic workers or menial laborers.

Ing Hay's partner, Lung On, was a savvy businessman and entrepreneur who had several thriving businesses and, reportedly, many white "girlfriends." Historians speculate that a large portion of Lung On's early business would have included creating false immigration documents to help Chinese people come to America. In the early days, when mobs of white men regularly swept the streets in drunken revelry aiming to shoot the neighbors they called "Chinese dogs" on sight, a business like Kam Wah Chung was more than just a store: it served as a communal fortress where miners and ranch hands, down from the hills to clean up and buy supplies, could drink tea, eat delicacies imported from China, smell the familiar smells of soy and cooking oil, play Pai Gow, and smoke opium in relative safety behind reinforced iron doors and windows. Poverty kept most of these men from returning to China, and suicide was quite common among Chinese who despaired of ever being able to return home.

In its heyday, John Day's Chinatown, then known as Tiger Town, supported approximately one thousand Chinese men. By 1900 the Chinese population of the town had dropped to only 114, again, almost all of them men. One historian claims that not a single baby was born to Chinese parents in Oregon until 1940—mostly because Chinese women found it almost impossible to enter the country legally, due to deliberate scheming by lawmakers.

Together, Lung On and Ing Hay ran their store and dispensary of Chinese medicine even after the Chinese population of John Day dwindled to almost nothing; they were able to stay in business by relying on white customers, a rare accomplishment in a time when the laws of the land were designed to keep Chinese from establishing a residential or financial foothold in America. Ing Hay was such an institution in the town of John Day that he was invited to become a member of the local Masonic Temple in the 1930s.

Lung On died in 1940. Hay, who was partially blind from drinking bad liquor, became depressed after losing his lifelong friend and did not want to carry on. A distant relation, Bob Wah, brought his family to Kam Wah Chung to care for Ing Hay and carry on the business. Bob Wah worked with Ing Hay as a medical practitioner and cared for him for many years. Eventually, Hay fell and broke his hip and had to be taken to Portland to have his bones reset; he never fully healed. Ing Hay lived in a nursing home for four years before his death in 1952. He died on a cold metal gurney in a western institution after devoting his life to the practice of eastern, holistic medicine. His funeral featured an elaborate coffin decorated with an arbor of wreaths, as well as a Masonic symbol made of flowers.

Most of Ing Hay's Chinese contemporaries who died in America left specific instructions that their bones be returned to China to be interred in an ancestral burial ground. Ing Hay and Lung On broke with that tradition, requesting to be buried permanently in John Day. Visitors to the old graveyard today will find Ing Hay and Lung On buried beside Bob Wah and his wife. These four graves are the only Chinese graves in the entire cemetery.

Perhaps the most interesting thing about Ing Hay and his friend Lung On is that despite all of the hostilities and difficulties they faced as early Chinese immigrants in Oregon, they still loved America and became American citizens as soon as they were legally able. They became so American, in fact, that both men rejected what, even today, is a major tenet of Chinese culture: sending money home to help support one's family. Both Ing Hay and Lung On received letter after letter from their families asking for money. Though both men were well-off by Chinese standards of the day, they sent almost no money home to their parents, wives, or children in the half-century that they thrived in America. When Ing Hay died, $23,000 in uncashed checks was found under his bed.

Of all the historic figures in this book, we know the most about Ing Hay's life. There is now a museum housed in Kam Wah Chung that shows exactly how he lived—entering Kam Wah Chung is like entering a time capsule. Bob Wah donated the building to the city in the late 1950s, but it remained locked and unused for almost twenty years. Rediscovered and reopened in the 1970s, the building became a museum, which is now run by Oregon State Parks. There is a book about Ing Hay (*China Doctor of John Day, Oregon*), as well as an extensive collection of historical documents in the Oregon State Archives. And yet, there is at least one aspect of Ing Hay's life that remains a mystery: why would a man so rooted in Chinese religious and cultural traditions ignore his family's poverty? I wrote his section of poems with this question central in my mind.

Notes on the Poems

Ing Hay: The Chinese scholars I consulted suggest that the name "Ing" was probably an Americanization of the Chinese surname "Ying." I have used Ing throughout, because the name is part of the American identity the man chose for himself.

From "After the Joss House Fire"
Joss House: A temple for worshipping household gods and praying for good luck. The term comes from the Portuguese word for God (*deos*, from the Latin, *deus*), which became part of the pidgin language spoken in Chinese ports of call. When Chinese people began settling in America and building small, community temples, Americans latched onto the pidgin word and Americanized it to become "Joss," which they believed to be the Chinese word for God.

Invocation

Maybe he does not want to be found—
I grow impatient with my pen.
Slow down, says a ghost.
Turn off the phones and drink your wine.

You think too much about yourself. China,
America, it doesn't matter who loves me.
Like an island in a river delta,
Kam Wah Chung was my country.

Glimpse me in the flame of a Buddha candle,
taste me in the fragrance of jasmine tea.
From the smoke-stained walls of my store
comes the living breath of memory:

Childhood in Taishan

Mother says 100,000 ghosts haunt our land—
when the harvest is good, she threshes and cries all day
   long—
she boils tree roots when the rice crop fails—
Hay, she tells me, *the mountains make us strong.*

The older boys play war with ribboned sticks—
Die, enemy!—they swirl like dragons on a page.
Mother, I say, *what is an enemy?*
Nothing, she says, *only monsters in another village.*

Planting Season

Time to plant the rice again. Pants clotted and wet,
I follow my father through fields, patching mud walls.
Grandfather's bones whisper from beneath a rock:
Only a bird can fly beyond these hills.

Market Day

I walk with my mother to the next village,
back bent low under cabbages and turnips.
While she trades for salt-fish and cloth,
an old man tempts me with his fortune sticks.

His baboon face made pale by rice powder,
his claw-hand pointing, he frightens me—
What will you do: starve, fight, or sail away?
His question, like lightning, cracks open the sky.

Crossing the Pacific

There are sacrifices of the heart we make,
limbs severed so the trunk will have life.
As the junk sets sail for Hong Kong,
there is a stranger waving—she is my wife,

baby in her arms, another on her back.
Return, husband, she pleads with her eyes.
Her dreams of gold stretch over the sea.
Next to her, my mother prays and cries—

her husband is leaving her too. He's retching
over the side. "Watch the horizon," the other men say.
In Hong Kong, we board an iron ship, its steam
like dragon's breath. Day fades into restless day.

In the rocking cabin, men play Pai Gow—
water rushing against the hull drowns all thought—
cooking smells from the night's meal hang heavy and
   thick—
my father moans from his makeshift cot—

I'm lost inside another seasick dream.
Lurching topside, I heave into the waves below,
where I find the ship besieged by whales,
monstrous bodies lit up by a ghost-green glow.

Gold Mountain

We arrived to find a few mad Taishanese
culling through the only land left unclaimed:
played-out mines, abandoned by white men.
My father returned home, goldless, ashamed.

I felt like a bird who'd fallen from the sky.
I huddled all winter with goldmad men
crouched like demons around a stove,
each one gripping his bowl. All except for one:

when Lung On talked of Oregon, I could feel
the pulse of the place glimmer and twitch
like a trout on the end of a bamboo pole.
We're going to be rich, Lung On said. *Really rich*.

Arrival at John Day, Oregon

Juniper stands dot the landscape, line the ridge tops.
Steps from here, a white man builds a white church.
Two geese come untied from their flock, cry over a cold
    river—
let them rest awhile beside the red alder, the water
    birch.

Becoming the China Doctor

I have always become what is needed—
a son, a husband, a father—with little effort or foresight.
This is how Oregon welcomed me—
a space opened and I moved into it.

Another wound in a broken body,
I was born to seek out sickness in others.
At first they called me a witch doctor,
but in suffering, all men are brothers.

Now, not just Taishan men, but ranchers—
even ranchers' wives—walk right in.
Perched awkwardly on my wooden stool,
they offer up the pain beneath their blue-lined skin.

At Kam Wah Chung

My friends come in from the hills tonight
hungry for human voices, the click of Mahjong tiles.
Is this the curse of Taishan?
Wherever we go, we dream of somewhere else.

Meanwhile, barbarians waste this land,
squander their timber, water, and stone,
shoot us like dogs in the street for sport,
eat meat bloody off the bone.

Last week they set the whole canyon ablaze.
Even now, a mob of white men clamors at the door.
We are used to iron shutters, fortified walls.
They imagine us, not quite human, crouched in our lair.

But tonight the beds are clean, and the stove is hot;
our iron bars will hold fast against attack.
Friends, drift sweetly in your opium dreams,
cross the ocean on a dragon's back.

Preparations for the New Year

All the lights in Tiger Town are lit, the long year coming
 to a close.
Lung On works over the abacus, figuring our debts and
 debtors.
Down in the barn, a Taishan boy cries, "Death loves a
 shining mark,"
before he leaps from his chair and drifts among the
 rafters.

Electric Leon

Lung On doesn't mind barbarian laws
forbidding our wives to come.
He finds women who like his Chinese face,
who go out dancing and call him Leon.

While his new machine plays Chinese opera,
Leon strings electric lights in the kitchen.
"Hay, you old monk," he cackles,
"Welcome to Gold Mountain."

I sit brewing tea from hibiscus flowers,
while Leon sells Pontiacs to white men.
He is everything we ever dreamed of:
Oh, America, behold your glorious son!

Garden Harvest

We eat moon cakes from San Francisco
to celebrate our little garden harvest.
Far from the puddle fields of childhood,
we're sloshed, and I'm drunker than the rest.

Fat Tony plays his flute, Monkey Tom and Lung On
jump like colts, boys in a world without girls.
Visible in moonlight, the Blue Mountains
keep us safe, like parents who still love us.

After the Joss House Fire

From the top of Old How's laundry,
a mourning dove makes his two-toned call.
Oh China, we are a ghost people,
wandering the ashes of our ruined temple.

Even now the dove reveals your secret,
China: you never meant to stay.
We'll send your bones home in a box;
America didn't want you anyway.

And poor Ing Hay, a straggler too besotted
to leave. I sit and wait for just one baby to be born,
sit and wait for this country to claim me,
sit and wait until there's no one left to mourn.

Letters from Home

A letter from my son reminds me I have a son.
He complains of the puddle fields, just like me.
He wants to come to Gold Mountain—
so many voices call across the sea.

Son, be no trouble!
That is the gift I gave my father.
Find a wife, make your own life,
leave an old man to his pleasure.

And Father, expect nothing from me—
that is the gift I give my son.
Your other boys will tend your grave—
I have become an American.

Precious Things

Even after Lung On dies, I offer incense, fruit, and wine.
Every day I sit by the radio, wait for patients to come,
surrounded by the artifacts of life: a bear claw in a
   wooden box,
Lung On's hair still resting in his comb.

I keep the lamp unceasingly lit,
the shrine decorated with paper flowers, red ribbon—
while his bones become the roots of the willow,
and his flesh becomes the dirt of Oregon.

Early Easter

Walking from the graveyard at dawn, I saw a demon
in the flaming willow. My friend and I
were two birds in the same nest. Without him,
I forget how to sing, how to fly.

The white men gather in their white church,
offering songs of praise and thanks.
This sudden thaw has me worried tonight
that Canyon Creek will overflow its banks.

Bob Wah Comes to Kam Wah Chung

Lung On is dead, but still I keep the store.
A man who calls me uncle comes to care for me.
His children try on my Stetson and dance in the
   courtyard,
while his wife unearths my stash of whiskey.

I begin to unravel—the fumes of the kerosene lamp
mix with opera from Lung On's phonograph—I keep
the old recordings stashed in a box with 6,000 lives
I saved. When I fall, the children find me broken
   in a heap.

Girl Wife

Broken and blind, I remember my girl wife:
smell, sweet and nutty as white lotus seed—
lips, two goji berries soaked in wine—
arms, slight and fragile as a reed.

I feel blood pulse beneath her skin,
the velvet-smooth petals of the rose,
she opens to me. My brothers snore
in the next room, somewhere a rooster crows.

The son we made is an old man now.
My own skin wrinkles like oolong tea.
Soon I'll be a ghost with no one to tend my bones,
while an old crone curses me across the sea.

Instructions to Bob Wah

Look at this stone-faced man, his features worn away by
	time,
his cowboy hat comical. He is too proud for one so old,
his hands too bony and stained with age,
his veins like mountain ridges, blue and cold and hard.

In the light of the naked bulb, a Taishan girl
smiles from a calendar on the wall.
Is it winter again? Bare trees reflected in still water,
the river about to freeze over. Ice on the branches will fall

and shatter like glass. We must catalogue these things,
the blue and white of winter, the lives I didn't save,
mysterious shadows lurking in rafters, a dried oak leaf,
and here, the words I want you to carve on my grave,

written on this little slip of rice paper, when you
bury me beside Lung On. And what's in that clay bowl,
the one with fish swimming on the side? Write it down,
boy! Even a single mustard seed can be useful!

Last Dreams

A dove cries from the roof of the Joss house this morning.
In my last dream, the noise becomes a flute.
Lung On brews tea, brings me the bowl.
If I don't open my eyes, I will continue to float—

my dreams have tricked me again—it's just Bob Wah's wife,
come to wake me for the trip to Portland.
The Joss house burned down years ago.
Old friend, I have to let go of your hand.

My fingers ache with cold, left all night outside the blanket.
Oregon before dawn is cool and quiet as the moon.
The roadway is empty, leading into the distance,
and here is Bob Wah with the station wagon—too soon,
   too soon,

they bundle me in the back, where I rattle and bounce
over the mountain pass. Now rain is splashing
on the rear windshield. This is not the death I wanted.
Old friend, old friend, is that you I hear laughing?

At the Nursing Home in Portland

The walls of the nursing home are too white,
the nurses won't let me smoke.
A young doctor in a white coat and glasses
with crablike fingers likes to grab and poke

and sting me with needles, his face grotesque
with pity. He imagines he'll never grow old.
"There you go, friend." He pats my arm. He is not
my friend, or he wouldn't make me lie so cold

on this metal table. My lungs fill with fluid.
From another room, a woman cries.
Can no one cover my body with blankets?
So this is how an old man dies.

Mary Elizabeth Jane Colter

1869–1958

Architect

M ARY COLTER WAS BORN IN Pittsburgh, Pennsylvania, in 1869. Her family moved to Colorado and California before settling in St. Paul, Minnesota, where Colter grew up. Colter was fascinated by art and design—especially Native American Indian drawings—from an early age. After her father died, Mary, then seventeen, convinced her mother Rebecca to send her to art school in San Francisco to learn a trade that could support the family. Rebecca, Mary, and Mary's older sister Harriet moved to Oakland, California, where they lived while Mary attended art school across the Bay. After graduation, Mary secured a teaching job back in St. Paul.

Mary Colter taught art and gave community lectures on architecture and design for almost fifteen years before she finally caught the attention of restaurateur and hotelier Fred Harvey, who was famous for his hospitality business along the Atchison, Topeka, and Santa Fe Railroad. Harvey hired Mary to design the store at one of his hotels. Later, he hired her as the architect of a new building on the south rim of the Grand Canyon. The purpose of this building was to showcase the Indian art collection that belonged to the Fred Harvey Company, and to sell Indian-made souvenirs to Harvey customers. Mary Colter called her design Hopi House and based it on the ruins of Hopi communities in Arizona.

When the Hopi House was complete, Harvey had no more work for Mary, so she secured a job in Seattle, working as a designer for the Frederick & Nelson department store. Harriet and Rebecca moved to Seattle with Mary, but during the following year, Rebecca died of pernicious anemia. Then, in 1910, when Mary Colter was forty-one, she was finally offered a full-time job with the Fred Harvey Company designing new buildings.

For the rest of her life, Mary Colter defined a new style of architecture (now called National Park Service Rustic) by designing buildings based on indigenous traditions. She often imagined histories for her buildings, which helped guide her to organic, idiosyncratic designs that looked as if they had existed for centuries. For one building, she imported cobwebs to make a room look ancient and lived-in. Whether they knew it or not, travelers and visitors to the West experienced the land and culture as defined by Mary Colter's sensibility. Her designs dotted the railroad lines from Chicago to Los Angeles.

I grew up two hours from Walt Disney World, and I spent many a day inside the Magic Kingdom surrounded by the make-believe settings of Main Street, USA, Fantasyland, Frontierland, Adventureland, and Tomorrowland—all designed by Disney's team of "Imagineers." I firmly believe these Imagineers took their cue from Mary Colter's design tradition. She took what was essential about a time, a people, and a culture, and distilled it down, articulated it, and created a space in which visitors could experience those essentials. What Mary Colter began as an art form has now become an industry. And yet her name is hardly known today, only fifty years after her death.

A small concentration of Mary Colter's designs still stands around the south rim of the Grand Canyon; this grouping includes Hopi House, Hermit's Rest, the Watchtower, the Lookout, and Phantom Ranch. Her favorite project, a hotel called La Posada in Winslow, Arizona—for decades used as an office building—has since been lovingly restored and is once again open to guests.

Very little is known about Mary Colter's personal life, except that she was devoted to her sister, Harriet, whom she supported financially. During her employment with the Fred Harvey Company, Mary divided her time between an apartment in Kansas City, Kansas; a house in Altadena, California, where Harriet lived and later died; and the railroad. After she retired, Mary moved to Santa Fe, New Mexico, where she died in 1958 at the age of eighty-eight.

I find it remarkable how little is remembered or written about Mary Colter's romantic life, especially given that she died less than fifty years prior to my writing. Even misanthrope Lewis Wetzel reportedly had a sweetheart, and we know York had a wife, as well as lovers among the tribal peoples he met during his journey west. Mary Colter's forceful personality and creative genius certainly would have attracted admirers. It is left to us to imagine who they might have been. I have taken certain liberties in imagining her romantic partners. None of my research indicated that Mary Colter was a lesbian; rather, it was the very lack of information about her personal life that led me to imagine that she might have been.

I imagined Mary Colter as a creative-obsessive, so I included several poems written in the *ghazal* and sestina forms, which rework single words again and again to expose new meanings. Other poems in the section, through formal rhyme schemes and concrete structures (i.e., the words on the page form a picture), mimic an architect's need to create order and harmony.

Notes on the Poems

From "La Posada"
La Posada: Spanish for resting place. In this case, the name of Mary Colter's favorite project, a hotel in Winslow, Arizona.

Sand painting: Sand paintings are a sacred art form to the Hopi people, who offer up these delicate, intricate works as prayers and requests in times of need or as an act of worship.

From "The Alaska-Yukon-Pacific Exposition"
The Alaska-Yukon-Pacific Exposition: A kind of regional World's Fair to promote the Pacific Northwest that took place in Seattle in 1909, during the time Colter was working for the Frederick & Nelson department store.

Hopi House: The first project Colter designed at the Grand Canyon for the Fred Harvey Company.

From "In Praise of Mimbreños"
Mimbreños: (also Mimbres) People who lived in the Membres Valley area of Arizona and New Mexico. Their art is distinctive for its geometric shapes and its black figures painted on white or cream-colored backgrounds.

From "The Architect"
The Architect is Frank Lloyd Wright.

From "Hopi's *Sipapu*"
Sipapu: Hopi folklore tells that the Hopi people were originally birthed from a *sipapu*, a hole hidden in the Canyon floor, and that their souls would pass back through after death.

From "Ifcroft"

Mimbres Bowls: Prehistoric artifacts made by the Mimbreños or Mimbres people.

From "Secrets"

Balolookong Rock: Balolookong is the name of a Hopi spirit who takes the form of a water serpent. Mary Colter placed a large rock, resembling the shape of a serpent's head, on the Watchtower.

Invocation

Teach me to read the markings
on the canyon wall, worn away by wind
and water, the stories you left untold
in drawings, rock outcroppings,
your histories unimagined.

Everything you saw, you synthesized—
whispering austerity of dry grasses,
the patterns of the plow in earth,
beads of water in a spider's web—
made it useful, stark, and light,

exacting in its randomness.
Come whisper your love songs to
the cracks in this stone, harmonious
as Earth's own music, made perfect
by their imperfections.

La Posada

Now I am old. My false teeth click
in rumbling automobiles.
Young men glare at me on dirt roads.

I put myself to bed with milk
and whiskey and hide the empty bottles
in the neighbors' dustbin.

Bodies of soldiers litter Europe.
I built a house for their dreams,
but they have chosen dreamless sleep.

Surrounded by the art of my life,
I beg my own sleep. La Posada dwindles
into finite pieces of desert sand.

Gods who dwell beneath the earth,
take me where each form holds meaning.
Accept the sand painting of my life—

the patterns have tried to worship you.
Who will come? Who will rub
the sands of my life into this loose flesh?

Sewer Inspector's Daughter

beneath the city, I draw caverns that form and serve
the earth we are defined by spaces
useful rock, layered
art
a second city ghosts the city,
the parts of us we flush away, water
from a leaving storm, flows, converges, toward cataracts

we walk above the charneled tunnels—arched, miracled
absolute forms of darkness
stone wall drips of
water
vanishing point of
This Great Country of Ours,
catacombs of stone, home cradled in the earth, Father,

Mother irons your clothes as a way of mourning
your absence leaves a space
I walk into your echo
life
underweaves
the continent I want to make
our way from Minneapolis opens west without you

The Railroad

Atchison, Topeka, and Santa Fe, the railroad
ricocheted against the tongue, a rhythm railroad.
In youth, I hungered West, sang the railroad's
whistle-clatter over land; I would ride the railroad,

seek the Indian villages I kept beneath my bed—
how many nights I fell asleep, lamp still burning,
taking one last look at those drawings. Mother scolded,
but she feared me, feared losing me to the railroad.

Born in Pittsburgh, how could I not have building
at my core? The smell of cut wood, coughed up
smoke of coke and ore, steel, source of the West.
Instead of blood, my veins ran fast with railroad.

I longed for life uncluttered by man's artifice.
San Francisco, perched on the land's thumb, offended me;
her houses pranced like showgirls dressed in finery.
Nights, my strained head pounded like the railroad.

I ignored the pain and looked for things I loved:
discrete green trees scattered summer's golden grasses,
winter fog rolled over coastal ranges, inevitable,
slow flood, terrifying like the thrill of the railroad.

When I first saw the Canyon, I heard her whisper
what she wanted, how to build her *kivas* (though
I didn't know the word yet). She said every man,
every thing had led to our meeting, even the railroad.

The Alaska-Yukon-Pacific Exposition

I watch from the windows of Frederick & Nelson,
captivity of glass, dress forms, and furniture;
Indians barter on the steps of the store.
Across the road, men are making a building; stone—

twenty floors of it—bearing down on workers,
who bow to the designs of an unkind god,
forcing wind into gusty channels, mixing blood,
bowls, totems, rushing nowhere.

City architects work toward the great expo,
la Renaissance Française, straight from New York.
Domed paeans to Europe, combed walkways fork
through crystal palaces with pools. An Eskimo

village in the amusement park troubles me:
way of life frozen in an igloo, museum piece
up for sale. Down in Arizona, my Hopi House
on the Canyon's rim offers a similar curiosity.

I, too, have built what's coming. I pace
behind my window dressing. Model Ts, identical,
rut the tortured roads, insects swarming from their hill.
A mountain in the distance sometimes shows its face.

Reading the News in Seattle

This year, I watch the sunless sky sap life from mother's skin
as she withers like fruit left too long in the bowl. My own skin
grows lined and creased, country to seek refuge from, strata
   of skin
on skin, sky on sky. Seattle's rain, a constant assault on skin,

becomes its own kind of desert. For the first time, I am old,
while China crowns a three-year-old emperor. Poor boy,
condemned by blood. As I grow orphaned, I grow free;
rivers flow from me, like Vesuvius shattering its skin.

Blind men see what they want—I reel with Picasso,
while critics decry *Les Demoiselles d'Avignon*, whores
in African masks. Help me see from every way at once.
Help me drink their bodies through my skin.

When metal, wood, and stone are not enough, when blood
drains from the buildings we make, we'll build ghost cities
with ghostly breath. Newspapers hail the end
of reliance on God's earth. Plastic, they say, is smooth as skin.

In Praise of Mimbreños

Like the Sioux drawings I hid in childhood
to spare them from my mother's cleansing
wrath against the smallpox

                        (I feared the death
of desire more), the breath each creature held,
stark horse against white paper,
village women clustered in bright wraps,

sacred figures against the ground of childhood;

so you, wild hare, as you ride your crescent into air:
I praise you for your arched back, defined form in space,
landscape given meaning by your lithe power.

The Architect

Has my life been so small, crisscrossing this West?
The Architect plans a city in Persia—atavistic ruins.

The Architect builds the way a man will build:
recreating himself, scattering women in ruins.

His edges cut like razor into rock;
societies fawn over One Man's ruins.

My students lionize the Architect with mimicry.
Mary, I whisper, look past them to Oraibi, Arizona's
   desert ruins.

Field Notes

Forms found in rock:

a woman in a bright-hued skirt
blows upon a horned flute—
she is betrothed to a stone god

with a bird-beaked nose
on the far wall
(his life longer than flesh)—

the Canyon their unhappy bed.
Also note: footprints of a three-toed man,
the small mouth of a fish,

ridges in rock—like petals,
like water, like my lover's hair—
the swirl of breasts,

marriage of stone on stone,
eye meets eye, lip meets lip,
arm encircles back, gathers

cascades of stone hair.
Stone bellies expel stone breath.
Centuries of upswelling,

terrifying depth of rock, strata,
form, the apparition of,
the tyranny of surfaces,

and in the distance comes
the bright boat of crescent moon,
the sound of wild hare laughing.

The World in Simplest Terms

        stark
            outline—
                    one bird
            on red
        stone

Three Buildings on the Canyon Rim

A lantern shows the way to Hermit's Rest—
rough arch (how carefully I chose the stones),
uneven wall (I made the men tear down the straight),
mission bell (authentically cracked),
its tone deadened (imperfection aching to be satisfied),
miles of cobweb (imported to signify age).

I made a spirit live there, a kind of mage
who left the world to find his rest
in the Canyon's wind and solitude. He satisfied
himself through rough handiwork. His stones
formed a crooked chimney; fingers, cracked
from cold and prayer, could not make it straight.

"The Watchtower ain't built straight."
Men laughed at my design on the page;
but I had flown the far desert, cracked
open secret places of the Hopi, pressed
my cheek against their weathered stones.
I understood their gods, what satisfied.

Upward reaching fist, aren't you satisfied?
I made the earth yearn straight
to sky. I made secrets hide beneath your stones
and prayers sleep upon the sacred stage
of your history. Within each *kiva* circle rests
the next mystery waiting to be cracked.

I planted weeds on the Lookout roof, cracked
and gullied with myriad rock. I was satisfied
when a woman couldn't tell my walls from the rest
of the world. Most days, you could see straight
across the Canyon, or down—from that vantage
travelers on burros looked small as stones.

Sometimes I see apparitions in the stones—
figures draped in gray shadow, faces cracked.
Sometimes memory conspires with age,
and the old love comes back to be satisfied.
I mistake the fog for smoke and can't see straight;
I want to throw myself against the Canyon's breast.

But I must build until the stones are satisfied.
The cracked bell of my body works against the straight
line of age. Until all forms are unified, I cannot rest.

Hopi's *Sipapu*

Canyon birthed the people from a red womb,
small opening in deepest earth.
When I am old, I will find the Canyon's secret
and rejoin her Spirit.

My bones will form upswellings
of new rock

as I break into form and function
beyond human mind,
a spirit dwelling,
pure architecture, Canyon's offspring of stone and light.

Ifcroft

Ifcroft, my Altadena home, sits like an empty bowl
now that you are dead, sister. Someone sent a bowl
of camellias for comfort. Your life was the china bowl
I formed myself against; I turned into a Mimbres bowl:

stark and useful, an outline of myself. In the Kodak
of you and me, your face is blurred behind mine.
I remember you that way, not like you were in life,
sharp-boned and drawn, your body a cracked bowl

that let the water seep out. Now I see that I built
homes for imaginary lives. Real lives do not last.
Even Gable and Lombard will die like the Indians
they come to gawk at. Mimbres buried their bowls

beneath the floor with their dead. Pottery for company,
useful in the afterworld. Artifacts become history.
Everything you made was light and useless, Harriet.
Should I bury you with your ribbons and bowls

of beads, your fingers lost in millinery? Nonsense
to believe an artifact reflects a people. Rather, see
one woman, lost in the lines and arcs of inner life,
her head bowed over the work of a bowl.

Harvey Girls

Between trains, Kansas air stood still
as if a tornado had just blown through
and left the whole world in silhouette:
Topeka flattened against deepening blue.
On my days off, I walked. "Hello, Miss,"
the Harvey Girls waved, dressed sweet

in Sunday clothes, swimming in wheat
with farm boys. Off-duty, unpinned, still
a good Harvey Girl played the perfect miss,
even entertaining workmen passing through,
but only just enough. At night, she blew
a kiss to distant love, a windowed silhouette.

One girl, Lucy, had a flat-nosed silhouette
and wore her hair in sheaves like wheat
or twisted snakes. I wanted to touch the blue
veins inside her wrist, lie near her, just lie still.
But she stayed formal, through and through—
Harvey girls knew their place and called me *"Miss*

Colter."* They didn't want to be dismissed.
But when Katie came, I watched her silhouette
against stars—she, the dark no light shone through.
She broke rules, took my hands in hers, sweet
with love; my skin rough and hardened by age. Still
she kept me. For my eyes, she called me "Liza-blue."

I watched her marry in her best dress, pale blue
with lace at the neck. Her brakeman said, "Miss,"
and tipped his hat goodbye to me. For a time, still,
when I saw a girl on the last car, in silhouette,
her face a dark spot against the twilight wheat,
I waved like a fool at the train roaring through.

In the desert, I think love might be through
with me. I am an old woman, just a tableau
really, of flesh on bone on sand. Now wheat
is just another color for stone. All my promise
spent on the Santa Fe line, walled silhouettes
expended. Night in the desert is so still.

The stars shoot holes through sky. I reach, miss.
Listen: rocks jut upward in blue silhouette.
In Kansas, wheat is waving, waving, then still.

Secrets

In the Watchtower, I left a hollow space beneath one stone. A dancer's feet could play it like a drum. Balolookong Rock hung from the outer wall, casting his spell. I saw men carry something inside their ribs that stirred and writhed like snakes—left by their fathers, awakened by war. Dancer, it's too late to raise the dead. No one comes to find the hollow place anymore, and the country has a serpent sleeping at its center. I died alone and dropped through levels of the Canyon to sleep there, patient as the rock.

Bibliography

Several institutions generously assisted my research for this project, including the West Virginia State Archives, the Ohio State Archives, the Oregon Historical Society, the Kam Wah Chung Museum, the Jefferson Library at Monticello, and the Monticello Center for Historic Plants. My sources included photographs and materials from vertical files and microfilm at these institutions.

I consulted many sources to compile these poetic histories. I am grateful to the following authors, filmmakers, scholars, and institutions for their careful research and assistance.

Lewis Wetzel

Allman, C. B. *Lewis Wetzel, Indian Fighter: The Life and Times of a Frontier Hero.* New York: Devin-Adair Co., 1961.

Carrol, George. "Lewis Wetzel: Warfare Tactics on the Frontier." *West Virginia History.* Volume 50 (1991), pp. 79–90. www.wvculture.org

Eckert, Allan W. *That Dark and Bloody River: Chronicles of the Ohio River Valley.* New York: Bantam Books, 1995.

Ellis, Edward Sylvester. *The Life and Times of Col. Daniel Boone: Hunter, Soldier, and Pioneer. With Sketches of Simon Kenton, Lewis Wetzel and Other Leaders in the Settlement of the West.* Philadelphia: Porter & Coates, 1884.

Lobdell, Jared C., editor. *Recollections of Lewis Bonnett, Jr. (1778–1850) and the Bonnett and Wetzel Families.* Maryland: Heritage Books, 1991.

Meyers, Robert Cornelius V. *Life and Adventures of Lewis Wetzel, the Renowned Virginia Ranger and Scout.* Philadelphia: J. E. Potter & Co., 1883.

Pierce, James P. "Lewis Wetzel, Dark Hero of the Ohio." *Early American Review.* Spring 1997. www.earlyamerica.com

Thornbrough, Gayle, editor. *Outpost on the Wabash, 1787–1791: Letters of Brigadier General Josiah Harmar.* Indianapolis: Indiana Historical Society, 1957.

York

Ambrose, Stephen. *Undaunted Courage: Meriwether Lewis, Thomas Jefferson, and the Opening of the American West*. New York: Simon & Schuster, 1996.

Betts, Robert B. *In Search of York: The Slave Who Went to the Pacific with Lewis and Clark*. Colorado: Colorado Associated University Press, 1985.

Millner, Darrell M. *York of the Corps of Discovery*. Portland: Oregon Historical Society, 2004.

Moulton, Gary, editor. *The Journals of the Lewis and Clark Expedition*. Lincoln: University of Nebraska Press, 1983.

Ronda, James P. *Lewis and Clark Among the Indians*. Lincoln: University of Nebraska Press, 1984.

Charity Lamb

Lansing, Ronald B. "The Tragedy of Charity Lamb, Oregon's First Convicted Murderess." *Oregon Historical Quarterly*, Volume 101, Number 1, Spring 2000.

Ing Hay

Barlow, Jeffrey and Christine Richardson. *China Doctor of John Day, Oregon*. Portland: Binford & Mort, 1979.

Chandler, Robert J. and Stephen J. Potash. *Gold, Silk, Pioneers & Mail: The Story of the Pacific Mail Steamship Company*. San Francisco: Friends of the San Francisco Maritime Museum Library, 2007.

Chen, Chia-lin. *A Gold Dream in the Blue Mountains: A Study of the Chinese Immigrants in the John Day Area, Oregon, 1870–1910*. Portland: Portland State University Thesis, 1972.

Chen, Chia-lin, trans. *Kam Wah Chung Company Papers, John Day, Oregon*. Portland: Oregon Historical Society, 1974.

Chinese American Voices: From the Gold Rush to the Present. Edited by Judy Yung, Gordon H. Chang, and H. Mark Lai. Berkeley: University of California Press, 2006.

Harrison, Henrietta. *The Man Awakened from Dreams: One Man's Life in a North China Village, 1857–1942.* Stanford: Stanford University Press, 2005.

Hsu, Madeleine. *Dreaming of Gold, Dreaming of Home: Transnationalism and Migration Between the United States and South China, 1882–1943.* Stanford: Stanford University Press, 2000.

Ivanhoe, Philip J. and Bryan W. Van Norden. *Readings in Chinese Classical Philosophy.* Indianapolis: Hackett Publishing, 2006.

McCunn, Ruthanne Lum. *Chinese American Portraits: Personal Histories, 1828–1988.* Seattle: University of Washington Press, 1996.

Mary Colter

Berke, Arnold. *Mary Colter: Architect of the Southwest.* New York: Princeton Architectural Press, 2002.

Grattan, Virginia L. *Mary Colter: Builder Upon the Red Earth.* Flagstaff: Northland Press, 1992.

Mary Jane Colter: House Made of Dawn (1997), Karen A. Bartlett writer, director, producer.

Poling-Kempes, Lesley. *The Harvey Girls: Women Who Opened the West.* New York: Paragon House, 1989.

OOLIGAN PRESS is a general trade press at Portland State University. In addition to publishing books that honor cultural and natural diversity, it is dedicated to teaching the art and craft of publishing.

As a teaching press, Ooligan makes as little distinction as possible between the press and the classroom. Under the direction of professional faculty and staff, the work of the Press is done by students enrolled in the Book Publishing graduate program at PSU. Publishing profitable books in real markets provides projects in which students combine theory with practice.

Ooligan Press offers the school and general community a full range of publishing services, from consulting and planning to design and production. Ooligan Press students, having already received important "real world" training while at the university and in various internship positions in the greater Portland area, are ideal candidates for jobs in the country's growing community of independent publishers.

This edition of *Killing George Washington* was produced by the following students on behalf of Ooligan Press:

ACQUISITIONS
Jason Evans
Katrina Hill

BOOK EDITING LEAD
Emilee Newman Bowles

EDITING GROUP
Rebecca Daniels
Kylin Larsson
Melissa Shore

COPYEDITING
Daniel Chabon
Ian VanWyhe
Mel Wells

OTHER EDITING ASSISTANCE
Elizabeth Anderson
Logan Balestrino
Tony Chiotti
Carly Cohen
McKenzie R. Gaby
Mike Hirte
Daniel Hubbell

Chris Huff
Amanda Johnson
Karen Kirtley
Malini Kochhar
Miala Leong
Gloria Lewis
Dehlia McCobb
Scott Parker
Megan Petersen-Kindem
Clara Settle
Leah Sims
Kari Smit
Emmalisa Sparrow
Rachael Spivey
Rita Tiwari
Megan Wellman
Parisa Zolfaghari

DESIGN
Kelley Dodd
Chelsea Harlan

MARKETING
Shannon Barraff
Carole Studebaker

Anne Jennings Paris has a BA in English Literature and an MFA in Creative Writing. Her poems have appeared in *Zyzzyva*, the *Cimarron Review*, and the *Pomona Valley Review*. She attributes her interest in American history to the stories told to her in childhood by her father, Bruce Jennings. Anne lives in the Portland area with her husband and son. *Killing George Washington* is her first book.

Breinigsville, PA USA
30 September 2009
225046BV00001B/5/P